Dear! Banana Bread Diary

(Volume 1)

Make An Awesome Month With 31 Best Banana Bread Recipes!

PuPaDo Family

Contents

Introduction

***

Hello,

Thank you for visiting **PuPaDo Family**!

Many years ago, each of us had a dream to possess a private house for our own when growing up! That house is a warm place which would keep our nice memories and make us think about first every time we feel tired of the busy modern life. That would also be the house for us to share together experiences and inspire desires. We do not share the same hobby. There are some love cooking, some others like traveling, or beauty care, etc.

PuPaDo Family was built from such dreams, thanks for the need of **spreading, sharing and inspiring experiences and desires**. If you have any desire, you can absolutely join our big **PuPaDo Family**, and we can sit close together and shorten all distances.

PuPaDo Cooking Family would be the starting chapter to be a gift for cooking lovers. No matter who you are, where you live, as long as you have an endless love for cooking, you would be a member of PuPaDo Cooking Family!

From the fact that I often write diaries to save every moment in life, especially whenever I walk into the kitchen, I make the series "**Dear, Diary**"! You are holding your hand the book "**Dear, Banana Bread Diary Volume 1**" in the series. I firmly believe that each dish always has an interesting story to keep, so that when I make it, or read what I have written, I will recall in my mind the memories. Therefore, each book in this series will not only a normal cookbook, but also a small diary of your own. In this diary you will note down experiences after failures, and keep little stories in your daily life and especially the final result after your "experiments" in the kitchen as well.

I am actually not a professional cook or cake baker. I even did not care about cooking until I left home to study abroad. From then on, I had to go to the kitchen and make meals myself. At first, it was like I was forced to cook, but gradually, it turned to a relaxed time after stressful studying hours in the class. Finally, I fell into love my kitchen and cooking uncontrollably.

One of the biggest values that I realize from the time I spend on my kitchen, cooking has the power to connect and promote love incredibly. To me, a batch of crispy and fragrant cake is the most effective remedy to soothe all the negative feeling. Not only for my own self, cooking is also a very good way to express the carefulness and love to the people around us. I hope that **PuPaDo Cooking Family** would not only be my own pretty kitchen, but also the inspiring place for other people toward cooking. And therefore, let's consider **PuPaDo Cooking Family** as your own kitchen and feel free to create in the family!

It is very nice that you have visited **PuPaDo Cooking Family** and read through this line. Hopefully, I would see you again in the kitchen more time later on. And I also hope "**Dear, Banana Bread Diary Volume 1**" would always be your companion in your pretty kitchen!

If you have time, let's leave some lines about yourself, or share your interesting stories, delicious dishes and memorable moments with us here!

PuPaDo Family.

List of Abbreviations

PuPaDo Family

PuPaDo Cooking

FOLLOW   ...

LIST OF ABBREVIATIONS

Tbsp(s).	Tablespoon(s)
Tsp(s).	Teaspoon(s)
C	Cup

Part 1: "Secret" For Perfect Quick Breads!

***

If I have to choose one of the most favorite time in a day, I am sure that it is morning. Why? Because in the morning, I can enjoy breakfast- my favorite meal of the day! One of the best breakfast I really enjoy and want to recommend for you are tasty slices of "quick bread" such as muffin, banana bread, cornbread, zucchini, waffles, pancake, etc. They ensure 3 things for a perfect breakfast that are quick, easy and delicious!

So, what are exactly quick bread? It is easy to explain. As their name "quick bread", they are very quick to prepare because they do not include yeast that often takes hours to rise. They use leaveners such as baking soda, sodium bicarbonate, baking powder, or cream of tartar for rising, instead of yeast. Generally, quick bread often involve flour, baking soda/ baking powder or both, eggs, milk, oil/butter. For the texture and flavor of quick bread, other ingredients such as nuts, fruits, sugars, and liquid are added into. Therefore, the texture of quick bread depends on the ingredients. But in general, they are often light, dense of fluffy, and moist.

1. Mixing method

Basing on the recipes and additional ingredients, people have their own way to mix ingredients together. However, there are three basic ways to make quick bread

- ✓ Creaming method: Beat and cream sugar and butter until they are fluffy and smooth. Then, add in the mixture liquid flavoring and eggs. Finally, fold dry ingredients and other liquids. This one is the best method for cakes because there are a lot of air pockets that are added into the mixture. Air pockets created by folding will keep the cakes fluffy and light.
- ✓ Muffin method: As the name, this one is the best when baking muffins. In the method, wet ingredients and dry ones are kept separated. At the very end of the process, they are combined until just incorporated.
- ✓ Shortening method: This final one is the best when baking pie crusts, biscuits, or scones. The method requires chilled fat (shortening or butter) to be cut into

dry ingredients that use a blender, or food processor, or fork. The texture of quick bread when using this method will be flaky due to chilled fat that melts while in the oven.

2. Types of batter

Depending on the recipes of quick bread, there are 3 types of batter with dry:liquid ratios that you can even use them to create your own quick bread recipes

- ✓ Stiff Dough: A {dry:liquis} ratio of this batter is {7:1} that makes the texture of quick bread very fluffy and light.
- ✓ Drop Batter: A {dry:liquis} ratio of this batter is {3:1} that makes the texture of quick bread moist but fluffy.
- ✓ Pour Batter: A {dry:liquis} ratio of this batter is {1:1} that is so much liquid in this type of batter. So, it will result in a very moist and dense baked good.

3. Tips for baking best quick bread

- ✓ Before you pour the batter, remember to grease the pans in order that the finished quick bread does not stick to the pans. (If you use high quality non- stick baking pans, skip the step)
- ✓ Do Not overmix the batter. The dry ingredients and the wet ones should only be combined until they are just incorporated, especially when baking muffins. Doing overmix batter will result in tunnels and big holes in the finished quick bread.
- ✓ As soon as the batter is mixed, pour it in the baking dish and place it in the preheated oven immediately in order that the quick bread rises appropriately (unless otherwise stated in a recipe).
- ✓ Keep an eye on the quick bread while baking, and remove it from heat when it turns golden brown. It may have a crack along the center of loaf bread but it is completely normal with quick bread since it is the character of this bread type.

- ✓ For a very moist quick bread, glaze it as soon as the bread is removed from the oven.
- ✓ Store loaf of quick bread in an airtight container for up to a few days.

Part 2: 31 Awesome Banana Bread Recipes

***

1. Banana Cranberry Bread

"With the leftover of cranberries sauce for Thanksgiving, I make this recipe, which is very tasty and moist."

*Servings: 24 | **Prep:** 15 m | **Ready In:** 1 h 30 m*

Ingredients

- 2 1/2 c white sugar
- 1 c shortening
- 3 eggs
- 3 mashed bananas
- 1 c cranberry sauce
- 1/2 c milk
- 1 tsp. vanilla extract
- 4 c all-purpose flour
- 1 1/2 tsps. baking soda
- 1 1/2 tsps. baking powder
- 1 tsp. ground cinnamon
- 1/2 tsp. ground nutmeg
- 1/2 c chopped walnuts

Directions

- Heat the oven to 350⁰F. Grease a thin layer on two 9x5 inch loaf pans.
- Mix shortening and sugar in a large bowl until light and fluffy. Blend with vanilla, milk, cranberry sauce, banana and eggs. Mix nutmeg, cinnamon, baking powder, baking soda and flour in another bowl. Use nuts to fold and transfer to the loaf pans.
- Bring to bake for 50-60 minutes. Let cool for 10 minutes and put into a wire rack for completely cooling down.

Nutrition Information

- Nutritionist's Calories: 292 kcal 15%
- Total Fat: 11.2 g 17%
- Carbohydrates: 45.4g 15%
- Protein: 3.7 g 7%
- Cholesterol: 24 mg 8%
- Sodium: 116 mg 5%

Note Me

2. Banana Nut and Ginger Bread

"This recipe is special due to the addition of beer. Replace raisins or currants for the dates if needed."

Servings: *24 |* ***Prep:*** *25 m |* ***Ready In:*** *1 h 25 m*

Ingredients

- 2 c packed brown sugar
- 1 c mashed bananas
- 2 eggs
- 1 tsp. vanilla extract
- 2 tbsps. vegetable oil (optional)
- 3 c all-purpose flour
- 2 tsps. baking soda
- 1 tsp. salt
- 1 1/2 tsps. ground cinnamon
- 1/2 tsp. ground allspice
- 1 tbsp. ground cardamom
- 1/2 tsp. ground cloves
- 2 c dark beer
- 1 1/2 c chopped walnuts
- 2 tbsps. all-purpose flour
- 2 c dates, pitted and chopped
- 2 tbsps. minced fresh ginger root

Directions

- Heat the oven to 350^0F. Grease a thin layer on two 9x5 inch loaf pans.
- Blend vanilla, eggs, banana and brown sugar in a large bowl. Add oil for more moist if necessary.

- Mix cloves, cardamom, all spices, cinnamon, salt, baking soda and 3 c flour in another bowl. Gradually mix the flour mixture with beer in the banana mixture.
- Toss with walnuts to the remaining flour. Blend with the dates and ginger. Add into the two loaf pans.
- Bring to bakes for 1 hour.

Nutrition Information

- Nutritionist's Calories: 246 kcal 12%
- Total Fat: 6.6 g 10%
- Carbohydrates: 44g 14%
- Protein: 3.9 g 8%
- Cholesterol: 16 mg 5%
- Sodium: 214 mg 9%

Note Me

3. Banana Nut Bread Baked in a Jar

"This is a great gift for friends and our relatives. Garnish before serving with label and a circle of Christmas fabric. This recipe can be made into other c=variants with different fruits and veggies."

*Servings: 24 | **Prep:** 10 m | **Ready In:** 1 h 5 m*

Ingredients
- 2/3 c shortening
- 2 2/3 c white sugar
- 4 eggs
- 2 c mashed bananas
- 2/3 c water
- 3 1/3 c all-purpose flour
- 1/2 tsp. baking powder
- 2 tsps. baking soda
- 1 1/2 tsps. salt
- 1 tsp. ground cinnamon
- 1 tsp. ground cloves
- 2/3 c chopped pecans

Directions
- Heat the oven to 325^0F. Grease a thin layer over 8 straight sided and wide mouth canning jars.
- Blend sugar, shortening in a large bowl. Mix with water, bananas and eggs. Add cloves, cinnamon, salt, soda, baking powder and flour in the mixture before adding bananas and stir with nuts.
- Transfer the mixture in the pint jars with half of the batter. Do not use lid for baking. Keep the rims clean.
- Bring to bake for 45 minutes. At the same time, sterilize the lids and rings in hot water.

- Take the cake out when it is done. Wipe rims of jars, put on lid and ring. When cake cools down, jars will seal. Put the jars on the counter and listen for it to "ping", press on the top of the lid. The cake is sealed when it does not move.
- Serve immediately or keep in the fridge for up to 1 week.

Note Me

4. Banana Nut Bread I

"This dish is really tasty with nuts and moisture."

*Servings: 24 | **Prep:** 10 m | **Ready In:** 1 h 10 m*

Ingredients
- 2 1/2 c white sugar
- 1 c shortening
- 3 eggs
- 1 1/2 c mashed bananas
- 3 c all-purpose flour
- 1 1/4 c buttermilk
- 1 1/2 tsps. baking soda
- 1 1/2 tsps. baking powder
- 1 tsp. vanilla extract
- 1/2 c chopped walnuts

Directions
- Heat the oven to 350ºF.
- Mix sugar and shortening together. Mix with eggs and beat well before adding vanilla, buttermilk and bananas to blend. Add soda, baking powder and flour before continue mixing up. Stir with nuts if necessary. Transfer to two 9x5 inch pans with thin greased layer.
- Bring to bake for 50-60 minutes, or you can use a toothpick for checking.

Nutrition Information
- Nutritionist's Calories: 256 kcal 13%
- Total Fat: 11.1 g 17%

- Carbohydrates: 37.1g 12%
- Protein: 3.3 g 7%
- Cholesterol: 24 mg 8%
- Sodium: 132 mg 5%

Note Me

5. Banana Nut Bread III

"The ingredient of butter makes the bread wonderful. It suits well in small loaf pans. Replace pecans with walnuts if you like."

Servings: 16

Ingredients
- 1 3/4 c all-purpose flour
- 2 tsps. baking powder
- 1/4 tsp. baking soda
- 1/2 tsp. salt
- 1 c white sugar
- 1/2 c chopped pecans
- 2 eggs
- 1 c mashed bananas
- 1/2 c vegetable oil
- 1 tsp. vanilla extract

Directions
- Heat the oven to 350⁰F. Grease and flour over 2 8x4 inch loaf pans and set aside.
- Mix sugar, salt, baking soda, baking powder and flour together before stirring with vanilla extract, oil, bananas, eggs and nuts.
- Transfer to pans and bring to bake for 45-60 minutes. Let cool on wire rack for 10 minutes. Take out.

Nutrition Information
- Nutritionist's Calories: 205 kcal 10%
- Total Fat: 10.1 g 16%
- Carbohydrates: 26.9g 9%

- Protein: 2.7 g 5%
- Cholesterol: 23 mg 8%
- Sodium: 162 mg 6%

Note Me

6. Banana Peanut Butter Bread

"This recipe can be used easily to make tasty bread in a short time. Serve for breakfast or your snack."

***Servings:** 15 | **Prep:** 15 m | **Ready In:** 1 h 25 m*

Ingredients

- 1/2 c butter, softened
- 1 c white sugar
- 2 eggs
- 1/2 c peanut butter
- 2 bananas, mashed
- 2 c all-purpose flour
- 1 tsp. baking soda
- 1/2 c chopped walnuts

Directions

- Heat the oven to 325^0F. Grease a light layer over a 5x9 inch loaf pan.
- Mix sugar and butter in a large mixing bowl. Beat well with eggs and stir with baking soda, flour, bananas and peanut butter. Use walnuts to fold and transfer to the prepared pan.
- Bring to bake for 70 minutes at 325^0F. Take out and let cool in a wire rack.

Nutrition Information

- Nutritionist's Calories: 266 kcal 13%
- Total Fat: 13.9 g 21%
- Carbohydrates: 32.1g 10%
- Protein: 5.5 g 11%

- Cholesterol: 41 mg 14%
- Sodium: 179 mg 7%

Note Me

7. Banana Walnut Bread

"Use it in your breakfast or snack."

Servings: *12* | ***Prep:*** *10 m* | ***Ready In:*** *45 m*

Ingredients

- 1 1/4 c all-purpose flour
- 1/2 c sugar
- 2 tsps. Argo® Baking Powder
- 1/4 tsp. salt
- 1 egg
- 3/4 c mashed bananas
- 1/2 c Mazola® Corn Oil
- 1/2 tsp. Spice Islands® Pure Vanilla Extract
- 1/2 c chopped walnuts
- As needed Mazola® Pure No-Stick Canola or Butter Flavored Cooking Spray (optional)

Directions

- Heat the oven to 350⁰F. Mix salt, baking powder, sugar and flour in a medium mixing bowl. Add vanilla, oil, bananas and egg in to whisk. Blend with flour mixture until moistened. Use walnuts to fold. Spray cooking spray over 8 ½ x 4 ½ loaf pan. Transfer batter into the pan.
- Bring to bake for 35-40 minutes, you can use a wooden pick for checking. Take out into a wire rack. Let cool for 10 minutes and serve warm or store it in an air-tight container.

Nutrition Information

- Nutritionist's Calories: 210 kcal 11%

- Total Fat: 13.1 g 20%
- Carbohydrates: 22.4g 7%
- Protein: 2.7 g 5%
- Cholesterol: 14 mg 5%
- Sodium: 135 mg 5%

Note Me

8. Banana Walnut Cornbread

"This cornbread recipe is the combination of bananas and nuts to keep in the fridge. A food processor can be used to puree the ingredients."

*Servings: 8 | **Prep:** 10 m | **Ready In:** 1 h*

Ingredients

- 2 tbsps. honey
- 2 bananas, mashed
- 1/4 c vegetable oil
- 1/2 c milk
- 2 tsps. vanilla extract
- 1 c cornmeal
- 1 c whole wheat pastry flour
- 1 tbsp. baking powder
- 1 tsp. baking soda
- 1/2 tsp. ground cinnamon
- 1 1/2 c chopped walnuts
- 1 banana, sliced

Directions

- Heat the oven to 350°F. Grease a thin layer over an 8x8 baking pan.
- Put the vanilla, milk, canola oil, mashed bananas with honey in a blender or food processor and puree until the mixture gets smooth.
- Blend cinnamon, soda, baking powder, whole wheat flour and cornmeal before stirring in flour mixture until smooth. Fold in sliced bananas and walnuts. Transfer into the prepared pan.
- Bring to bake for 40-50 minutes.

Nutrition Information

- Nutritionist's Calories: 381 kcal 19%
- Total Fat: 22.6 g 35%
- Carbohydrates: 41.2g 13%
- Protein: 7.2 g 14%
- Cholesterol: 1 mg < 1%
- Sodium: 292 mg 12%

Note Me

9. Banana Walnut Flax Seed Bread

"This bread will be really flavorful with walnuts and flax seeds. It is very nutritious, tender and moist but not too sweet."

Servings: *20* | ***Prep:*** *30 m* | ***Ready In:*** *1 h 50 m*

Ingredients

- 2 c whole wheat flour
- 1 c flaxseed meal
- 1/4 c wheat germ
- 2 tsps. baking soda
- 1 tsp. ground cinnamon
- 1/3 tsp. sea salt
- 2 c chopped walnuts
- 4 eggs
- 2 c brown sugar
- 2/3 c sunflower seed oil
- 1/3 c roasted walnut oil
- 1/4 c plain yogurt
- 5 large ripe bananas, coarsely mashed, or more to taste
- 2 tsps. vanilla extract

Directions

- Heat the oven to 325⁰F. Use butter to grease 2 8x4 inch loaf pans.
- Blend salt, cinnamon, baking soda, wheat germ, flaxseed meal and whole wheat flour in a large bowl. Stir with walnuts.
- Beat brown sugar and eggs together in another bowl with an electric mixer for 3 minutes. Add yogurt, walnut oil and sunflower seed oil and blend well. Stir them with vanilla extract and mashed bananas.

- Blend the egg mixture into dry ingredients and mix until moistened. Divide the batter into two halves in the two loaf pans.
- Bring to bake for 75 minutes, you can use a toothpick for checking, and then take out, let stand for 5 minutes and let cool on wire racks.

Nutrition Information
- Nutritionist's Calories: 380 kcal 19%
- Total Fat: 22.4 g 34%
- Carbohydrates: 42.5g 14%
- Protein: 6.6 g 13%
- Cholesterol: 37 mg 12%
- Sodium: 181 mg 7%

Note Me

10. Banana Wheat Bread

"Very easy to process with healthy and tasty ingredients. It is my favorite breakfast of all time."

Servings: 12

Ingredients

- 2 c whole wheat flour
- 1/4 c wheat germ
- 1 tsp. salt
- 1 tsp. baking soda
- 1 1/2 c mashed bananas
- 1/4 c vegetable oil
- 1/2 c honey
- 2 eggs
- 1 tsp. vanilla extract
- 1/2 c chopped pecans

Directions

- Grease a thin layer over a 9x5 inch loaf pan. Heat the oven to 350^0F.
- Blend oil, mashed bananas, eggs, vanilla and honey in a bowl.
- Mix baking soda, salt, wheat germ and flour in a large bowl. Blend well with dry ingredients and put together with the banana mixture and mix until smooth. Stir with nuts and transfer the batter into the pan.
- Bring to bake for 1 hour. Let cool in a wire rack.

Nutrition Information

- Nutritionist's Calories: 232 kcal 12%

- Total Fat: 9.7 g 15%
- Carbohydrates: 34.6g 11%
- Protein: 5.1 g 10%
- Cholesterol: 31 mg 10%
- Sodium: 313 mg 13%

Note Me

_____

_____

_____

_____

_____

_____

_____

_____

_____

_____

_____

_____

_____

11. Banana-Zucchini Bread

"My two favorites are blended in this recipe: zucchini bread and banana nut bread. It is very flavorful and you can feel it in every bite."

*Servings: 20 | **Prep:** 15 m | **Ready In:** 1 h 5 m*

Ingredients

- 3 eggs
- 3/4 c vegetable oil
- 2/3 c packed brown sugar
- 1 c white sugar
- 1 c grated zucchini
- 2 bananas, mashed
- 2 tsps. vanilla extract
- 3 1/2 c all-purpose flour
- 1 tbsp. ground cinnamon
- 1 1/2 tsps. baking powder
- 1 tsp. baking soda
- 1 tsp. salt
- 1/2 c dried cranberries
- 1/2 c chopped walnuts

Directions

- Heat the oven to 325^{0}F. Grease a thin layer on two 8x4 inch bread loaf pans.
- Whisk eggs in a large bowl until yellow and fluffy. Blend with vanilla, bananas, grated zucchini, white sugar, oil and brown sugar. Add nuts and cranberries to mix. Divide the batter in the prepared loaf pans.
- Bring to bake for 50 minutes. You can use a toothpick to check. Let cool in a wire rack. Take our and serve.

Nutrition Information

- Nutritionist's Calories: 272 kcal 14%
- Total Fat: 11.1 g 17%
- Carbohydrates: 40.2g 13%
- Protein: 3.9 g 8%
- Cholesterol: 28 mg 9%
- Sodium: 230 mg 9%

Note Me

12. Bangin' Banana Bread

"This bread is very flavorful, fluffy and moist with ingredients of macadamia nuts."

***Servings:** 12 | **Prep:** 15 m | **Ready In:** 1 h 25 m*

Ingredients

- 1/2 c butter, at room temperature
- 1/2 c white sugar
- 2 eggs, at room temperature
- 2 1/2 c pureed ripe bananas
- 1 1/4 tsps. baking soda
- 1/2 tsp. baking powder
- 1/4 tsp. kosher salt
- 1/2 tsp. vanilla extract
- 2 c all-purpose flour
- 1/2 c coarsely chopped macadamia nuts

Directions

- Heat the oven to 350^{0}F. Grease a thin layer over a 9x5 inch loaf pan.
- Mix sugar and butter together in a mixing bowl with an electric mixer. Whisk eggs and pour on the mixture of vanilla extract, salt, baking powder, baking soda and eggs. Sift with flour and blend with hands until smooth. Add macadamia nuts in the batter and fold.
- Transfer the batter into the prepared pan and bring to bake for 60-65 minutes.
- Take out and let rest for 10 minutes. Turn out from the pan.

Nutrition Information

- Nutritionist's Calories: 270 kcal 14%
- Total Fat: 13.1 g 20%
- Carbohydrates: 35.9g 12%
- Protein: 4.2 g 8%
- Cholesterol: 51 mg 17%
- Sodium: 259 mg 10%

Note Me

13. Basic Fruit Bread Recipe

"You can use any nuts, spices, veggies or fruits that you wish."

***Servings:** 10 | **Prep:** 10 m | **Ready In:** 50 m*

Ingredients
- 3 c all-purpose flour
- 2 tsps. baking powder
- 1 tsp. baking soda
- 1/2 tsp. salt
- 1 c white sugar
- 1/2 c vegetable oil
- 2 eggs
- 1 c shredded apple
- 3/4 c chopped walnuts
- 1/2 tsp. vanilla extract

Directions
- Heat the oven to 350^{0}F. Grease a thin layer over a 4 ½ x 8 ½ inch loaf pan.
- Blend vanilla, walnuts, apple, eggs, oil, sugar, salt, soda, baking powder and flour until moistened.
- Bring to bake for 4 ½ x 8 ½ inch loaf pan for 35-40 minutes.

Nutrition Information
- Nutritionist's Calories: 391 kcal 20%
- Total Fat: 18.1 g 28%
- Carbohydrates: 52.1g 17%
- Protein: 6.5 g 13%
- Cholesterol: 37 mg 12%

- Sodium: 357 mg 14%

Note Me

_____

_____

_____

_____

_____

_____

_____

_____

_____

_____

_____

_____

_____

14. Best Ever Banana Bread

"This is the tastiest banana bread I have tried. It is very moist and freezes well. Bring to bake in 3 separate loaf pans with shortening the baking time."

Servings: 12

Ingredients
- 2 eggs, beaten
- 1/3 c buttermilk
- 1/2 c vegetable oil
- 1 c mashed bananas
- 1 1/2 c white sugar
- 1 3/4 c all-purpose flour
- 1 tsp. baking soda
- 1/2 tsp. salt
- 1/2 c chopped pecans (optional)

Directions
- Heat the oven to 325^0F. Use non-stick spray coating to spray a 9x5 inch loaf pan.
- Mix with bananas, oil, buttermilk and eggs.
- Blend together with salt, baking soda, flour and sugar before adding to the banana mixture and pecans.
- Transfer to the loaf pan and bring to bake for 80 minutes. You can use a toothpick to check.

Nutrition Information
- Nutritionist's Calories: 307 kcal 15%
- Total Fat: 13.6 g 21%
- Carbohydrates: 44.2g 14%

- Protein: 3.8 g 8%
- Cholesterol: 31 mg 10%
- Sodium: 221 mg 9%

Note Me

15. Best Hawaiian Banana Nut Bread

"From some other related recipe, I thought about this combination for bread. I am not very experienced, but it is really tasty. You must try."

Servings: *12* | ***Prep:*** *30 m* | ***Ready In:*** *2 h 10 m*

Ingredients

- 2 c all-purpose flour
- 1 1/4 c white sugar
- 1 tbsp. light brown sugar
- 3/4 tsp. baking soda
- 3/4 tsp. ground cinnamon
- 1/2 tsp. baking powder
- 1/2 tsp. salt
- 1 1/3 c mashed bananas
- 2/3 c canola oil
- 2/3 c crushed pineapple, drained
- 2/3 c flaked coconut
- 1/4 c chopped walnuts
- 1/4 c chopped macadamia nuts
- 2 eggs, well beaten
- 4 tsps. applesauce
- 1 1/2 tsps. vanilla extract
- 1 tsp. lemon extract
- 1/2 tsp. coconut extract
- 2 tbsps. butter, at room temperature
- 1/4 c white sugar
- 1/4 c chopped walnuts
- 1/4 c chopped macadamia nuts
- 1 tsp. milk

Directions

- Heat the oven to 350⁰F. Grease a thin layer over a 9x5 inch loaf pan.
- Blend salt, baking powder, cinnamon, baking soda, brown sugar, 1 ¼ c sugar and flour in a large bowl. Stir with coconut extract, lemon extract, vanilla extract, applesauce, eggs, ¼ c macadamia nuts, ¼ c walnuts, flaked coconut, pineapple, canola oil and mashed banana into the flour mixture. Transfer the batter in the loaf pan.
- Bring to bake for 70-80 minutes. Let cool for 10 minutes and let cool in a wire rack for 20-30 minutes.
- Mix milk, ¼ c macadamia nuts, ¼ c walnuts and ¼ c white sugar in a bowl together. Spread on the top of bread in a wire rack.

Nutrition Information

- Nutritionist's Calories: 441 kcal 22%
- Total Fat: 24.1 g 37%
- Carbohydrates: 54g 17%
- Protein: 4.9 g 10%
- Cholesterol: 36 mg 12%
- Sodium: 235 mg 9%

Note Me

16. Black Sesame and Walnut Banana Bread

"With the special ingredients, I believe that it will be your favorite after once trying time. I make it twice a week as a habit."

***Servings:** 4 |* ***Prep:** 15 m |* ***Ready In:** 50 m*

Ingredients

- 3/4 c all-purpose flour
- 1/2 tsp. baking soda
- 1/2 tsp. baking powder
- 1/2 tsp. ground cinnamon (optional)
- 1/4 tsp. ground nutmeg (optional)
- 1/4 tsp. salt
- 1 large banana, mashed
- 1/4 c white sugar
- 1/4 c packed brown sugar
- 1 egg white
- 2 tbsps. milk
- 1 tbsp. canola oil
- 1/2 tsp. vanilla extract
- 1/3 c black sesame seeds
- 1/3 c chopped walnuts

Directions

- Heat the oven to 350⁰F. Grease a thin line over a loaf pan.
- Mix salt, nutmeg, cinnamon, baking powder, baking soda and flour in a bowl. Add vanilla extract, canola oil, milk, egg white, brown sugar, white sugar and banana in another bowl and stir until the mixture gest moisture. Fold walnuts and sesame seeds in the batter and pour into the prepared loaf pan.

- Bring to bake for 35-40 minutes and let cool before transferring to a wire rack.

Nutrition Information
- Nutritionist's Calories: 389 kcal 19%
- Total Fat: 16.4 g 25%
- Carbohydrates: 56.8g 18%
- Protein: 7.6 g 15%
- Cholesterol: < 1 mg < 1%
- Sodium: 386 mg 15%

Note Me

---

17. Blueberry Banana Nut Bread

"This recipe is very useful to make a tasty and moist bread. Add some lemon curd if you like."

***Servings:** 12 | **Prep:** 20 m | **Ready In:** 2 h 30 m*

Ingredients
- 1 1/2 c fresh blueberries
- 2 tbsps. cake flour
- 1/2 c steel-cut oats
- 1/2 c chopped pecans
- 1 1/2 c cake flour
- 3 tbsps. cake flour
- 1 tsp. baking soda
- 1/4 tsp. salt
- 1/2 c white sugar
- 1/2 c brown sugar
- 1/4 c Greek yogurt
- 1/4 c applesauce
- 2 eggs
- 1 tsp. vanilla extract
- 1 c mashed banana
- 2 tbsps. cold butter
- 1/4 c brown sugar

Directions
- Heat the oven to 350⁰F. Grease a thin layer with flour over a 4 ½ x 8 ½ inch loaf pan.
- Mix with blueberries for coating with 2 tbsps. cake flour.
- Blend with salt, baking soda, 1 ½ c and 3 tbsps. cake flour, pecans, oats and coated blueberries in a bowl.

- Mix apple sauce, Greek yogurt, ½ c brown sugar and white sugar in a large bowl until light and fluffy. Add eggs and beat it after each addition with mashed banana and vanilla extract.
- Add blueberry and flour mixture in the yogurt mixture and blend well until moistened. Spoon out the batter on the prepared pan. Divide the batter into ¼ c brown sugar in a small bowl and sprinkle over the batter.
- Bring to bake for 55 minutes. Let cool in the pan for 15 minutes and transfer to a rack for complete cooling, roughly 1 hour.

Nutrition Information
- Nutritionist's Calories: 265 kcal 13%
- Total Fat: 7.2 g 11%
- Carbohydrates: 46.8g 15%
- Protein: 4.7 g 9%
- Cholesterol: 37 mg 12%
- Sodium: 185 mg 7%

Note Me

_____

_____

_____

_____

_____

_____

_____

_____

_____

_____

_____

_____

_____

18. Brown Sugar Banana Nut Bread I

"This bread recipe is the combination of many flavors to make up the sweetness and deliciousness."

***Servings:** 12 | **Prep:** 15 m | **Ready In:** 1 h 15 m*

Ingredients

- 1/2 c butter, softened
- 1 c brown sugar
- 2 eggs
- 1 tbsp. vanilla extract
- 4 very ripe bananas, mashed
- 2 c all-purpose flour
- 3 tsps. baking powder
- 1/2 tsp. salt
- 1/2 c chopped walnuts

Directions

- Heat the oven to 350⁰F. Grease a thin layer over a 9x5 inch loaf pan.
- Mix sugar and butter in a large bowl until light and fluffy. Beat with eggs and stir in banana and vanilla. Mix salt, baking powder and flour together in another bowl.
- Blend the two mixtures together and stir to combine. Fold in walnuts and transfer the batter into the prepared pan.
- Bring to bake for 1 hour.

Nutrition Information

- Nutritionist's Calories: 273 kcal 14%
- Total Fat: 12.1 g 19%

- Carbohydrates: 37.9g 12%
- Protein: 4.5 g 9%
- Cholesterol: 51 mg 17%
- Sodium: 257 mg 10%

Note Me

19. Cardamom Banana Bread

"The fragrance makes this bread better than the pure banana bread. Replace cardamom with ground nutmeg if you wish. Without refrigeration, this bread can be kept for 5 days."

***Servings:** 12 | **Prep:** 20 m | **Ready In:** 1 h 20 m*

Ingredients
- 2/3 c raisins
- 1/3 c dark rum
- 3 ripe bananas, mashed
- 3/4 c packed brown sugar
- 1/3 c canola oil
- 2 eggs
- 1 c all-purpose flour
- 3/4 c whole wheat flour
- 1 tsp. baking powder
- 1 tsp. baking soda
- 1 tsp. salt
- 1 tsp. ground cardamom
- 1/2 c chopped walnuts, toasted

Directions
- Heat the oven to 350^0F. Grease a thin layer over a 9x5 inch loaf pan.
- Blend rum and raisins together in a small saucepan. Cook until simmering and remove from heat. Let cool for 10 minutes.
- Blend eggs, canola oil, brown sugar and mashed bananas in a large bowl with an electric mixer for 1 minutes. Mix with ground cardamom, salt, baking soda, baking powder, whole wheat flour

and all-purpose flour with a spoon until well blended. Add walnuts, rum with raisins. Transfer the batter into the prepared pan.
- Bring to bake for 50-60 minutes. Let cool and take out of the pan.

Nutrition Information
- Nutritionist's Calories: 281 kcal 14%
- Total Fat: 10.6 g 16%
- Carbohydrates: 40.9g 13%
- Protein: 4.5 g 9%
- Cholesterol: 31 mg 10%
- Sodium: 346 mg 14%

Note Me

20. Creamy Banana Bread

"This recipe has been adapted by me for several years. With the addition of banana, this bread is my family's favorite. With cream cheese and bananas, this bread is moist enough to serve in meal."

Servings: 16 | Prep: 30 m | Ready In: 1 h 15 m

Ingredients

- 1/2 c margarine, softened
- 1 (8 ounce) package cream cheese, softened
- 1 1/4 c white sugar
- 2 eggs
- 1 c mashed bananas
- 1 tsp. vanilla extract
- 2 1/4 c all-purpose flour
- 1 1/2 tsps. baking powder
- 1/2 tsp. baking soda
- 3/4 c chopped pecans
- 2 tbsps. brown sugar
- 2 tsps. ground cinnamon

Directions

- Heat the oven to 350°F. Grease and flour two 8x4 inch loaf pans.
- Mix cream cheese and margarine together and add sugar before mixing evenly until fluffy and light. Add eggs and beat after each addition. Stir with vanilla and mashed bananas. Blend with baking soda, baking powder and flour until the batter gets moist.
- Blend cinnamon, 2 tbsps. brown sugar and chopped pecans in a small bowl.
- Divide the batter into two halves and put into the prepared pans. Spread the pecan mixture on top and then the remaining batter.

- Bring to bake for 45 minutes.

Nutrition Information
- Nutritionist's Calories: 289 kcal 14%
- Total Fat: 15.1 g 23%
- Carbohydrates: 35.5g 11%
- Protein: 4.4 g 9%
- Cholesterol: 39 mg 13%
- Sodium: 213 mg 9%

Note Me

21. Dad's Banana Nut Bread

"This recipe is originally from my father. Serve it with fruits or coffee in the breakfast is the best. The flax seed makes great texture and flavor."

***Servings:** 16 |* ***Prep:** 20 m |* ***Ready In:** 2 h 20 m*

Ingredients

- 1/2 c butter, softened
- 1 c white sugar
- 2 eggs
- 2 very ripe bananas, mashed
- 1 c self-rising flour
- 1/4 c flax seed meal
- 1/2 c chopped walnuts (optional)

Directions

- Heat the oven to 325⁰F. Grease a thin layer over a 9x5 inch loaf pan.
- Mix sugar and butter with an electric mixer in a mixing bowl until light and fluffy.
- Beat the eggs and add bananas to blend one at a time.
- Blend flax seed meal and self-rising flour well and fold with walnuts.
- Transfer onto the prepared pan.
- Bring to bake for 20 minutes for muffins and 1 hour for a loaf. Let cool for 10 minutes and take out to a wire rack for complete cooling.

Nutrition Information

- Nutritionist's Calories: 182 kcal 9%

- Total Fat: 9.6 g 15%
- Carbohydrates: 22.7g 7%
- Protein: 2.7 g 5%
- Cholesterol: 39 mg 13%
- Sodium: 150 mg 6%

Note Me

22. Delicious Raisin Nut Banana Bread

"The blending of the ingredients is just great. Use raisin nut bran with tasty nut is my habit. You should try and enjoy it yourself."

***Servings:** 12 | **Prep:** 15 m | **Ready In:** 1 h 10 m*

Ingredients

- 2 c raisin nut bran cereal
- 1/2 c milk
- 1 1/2 c all-purpose flour
- 3 1/2 tsps. baking powder
- 1 tsp. baking soda
- 1/4 tsp. salt
- 1 c mashed ripe banana
- 1/2 c white sugar
- 1/4 c brown sugar
- 1/4 c vegetable oil
- 1 egg

Directions

- Heat the oven to 350^{0}F. Grease a thin layer over a 9x5 inch loaf pan.
- Mix milk with raisin nut bran cereal in a bowl and let stand for 5 minutes.
- Blend salt, baking soda, baking powder and flour in a large bowl. Mix egg, vegetable oil, brown sugar, sugar and mashed banana in another bowl. Add the cereal mixture into the banana mixture and stir well until combined. Transfer to the prepared pan.
- Bring to bake for 50-55 minutes and let cool before slicing.

Nutrition Information

- Nutritionist's Calories: 204 kcal 10%
- Total Fat: 6.1 g 9%
- Carbohydrates: 35.2g 11%
- Protein: 3.5 g 7%
- Cholesterol: 16 mg 5%
- Sodium: 311 mg 12%

Note Me

23. Double Banana Nut Bread

"Your guests will love to taste this moist and dense banana nut bread. It goes well with low or high altitude so you will enjoy it without any hesitation."

***Servings:** 24 | **Prep:** 20 m | **Ready In:** 1 h 35 m*

Ingredients
- 1 1/3 c vegetable oil
- 2 c white sugar
- 4 eggs, whisked
- 5 c mashed bananas
- 1 tbsp. lemon juice
- 4 c all-purpose flour
- 2 tbsps. baking powder
- 1 tsp. salt
- 2 c chopped walnuts

Directions
- Heat the oven to 350⁰F. Grease a thin layer over two 9x5 inch loaf pans.
- Stir well eggs with sugar and vegetable oil until creamy and smooth in a bowl.
- Mix mashed bananas and lemon juice in another bowl and mix into oil mixture until blended.
- Blend salt, baking powder and flour in another bowl and mix with the wet mixture with an electric mixer. Fold in walnuts and pour batter into two loaf pans.
- Bring to bake for 75 minutes.

Nutrition Information

- Nutritionist's Calories: 366 kcal 18%
- Total Fat: 19.7 g 30%
- Carbohydrates: 45g 15%
- Protein: 5.2 g 10%
- Cholesterol: 31 mg 10%
- Sodium: 232 mg 9%

Note Me

24. Extreme Banana Nut Bread 'EBNB'

"My mom has taught me this recipe of banana nut bread. All members in my family love it. Note that EBNB may be habit forming. Adjust the taste with your available ingredients. You can use butter, shortening or oil. Combine with brown or white sugar if needed."

***Servings:** 24 | **Prep:** 20 m | **Ready In:** 1 h 30 m*

Ingredients

- 2 c all-purpose flour
- 1 tsp. salt
- 2 tsps. baking soda
- 1 c butter or margarine
- 2 c white sugar
- 2 c mashed overripe bananas
- 4 eggs, beaten
- 1 c chopped walnuts

Directions

- Heat the oven to 350ºF. Grease and flour over two 9x5 inch loaf pans.
- Mix baking soda, salt and flour together in a large bowl. Blend sugar, margarine and butter in another bowl. Add walnuts, eggs and bananas to stir until well blended. Divide the batter into two loaf pans.
- Bring to bake for 60-70 minutes. Let cool for 5 minutes at least. Move to a cooling rack and wrap in aluminum foil to keep the moisture. Or you can keep in the fridge for 2 hours and serve.

Nutrition Information

- Nutritionist's Calories: 232 kcal 12%
- Total Fat: 11.9 g 18%
- Carbohydrates: 29.7g 10%
- Protein: 3.2 g 6%
- Cholesterol: 51 mg 17%
- Sodium: 268 mg 11%

Note Me

25. Family Banana Nut Bread Recipe

"My Dad taught me about this recipe. You will love it."

Servings: *10* | ***Prep:*** *20 m* | ***Ready In:*** *2 h 35 m*

Ingredients

- 1 (8 ounce) package cream cheese, softened
- 1 c white sugar
- 1/2 c butter
- 2 eggs, well-beaten
- 2 ripe bananas, mashed
- 2 1/4 c all-purpose flour
- 1 1/2 tsps. baking powder
- 1/2 tsp. baking soda
- 1 c chopped walnuts

Directions

- Heat the oven to 350⁰F. Add a greasy layer over a 9x5 inch loaf pan.
- Mix banana, eggs, butter, sugar and cream cheese in a large bowl until smooth. Stir with walnuts, baking soda, baking powder and flour until well combined. Transfer the batter into a loaf pan.
- Bring to bake for 75 minutes. Let cool for 10 minutes and taking onto a wire rack.

Nutrition Information

- Nutritionist's Calories: 450 kcal 22%
- Total Fat: 25.9 g 40%
- Carbohydrates: 49.3g 16%
- Protein: 7.8 g 16%

- Cholesterol: 82 mg 27%
- Sodium: 281 mg 11%

Note Me

26. Favorite Banana Blueberry Quick Bread

"The moist bread is very easy to make in a short time. People keep asking me for the recipe. Remember that you should thaw the frozen blueberries in the microwave for 3 minutes while at the same time, increase the amount of blueberries to ¾ c."

***Servings:** 12 | **Prep:** 25 m | **Ready In:** 1 h 25 m*

Ingredients

- 1/2 c fresh blueberries
- 1 5/8 c all-purpose flour
- 1/2 c quick cooking oats
- 1/2 c chopped pecans
- 1 tsp. baking soda
- 1/4 tsp. salt
- 1/2 c shortening
- 1 c white sugar
- 2 eggs
- 1 c mashed bananas

Directions

- Heat the oven to 350⁰F. Grease and flour a 9x5 inch loaf pan.
- Toss blueberries in 2 tbsps. flour in a medium bowl. Stir blueberries gently with oats, nuts, salt, 1 ½ c flour and baking soda.
- Cream shortening in a large bowl. Add sugar gradually in the bowl and stir until fluffy and light. Break eggs and mix with the mixture one at a time and beat well after each addition. Blend with mashed banana and blueberry mixture and cream until moistened. Spoon the batter to the prepared pan.

- Bring to bake for 50-55 minutes. Let cool in pan for 10 minutes and take out to a wire rack to cool completely.

Nutrition Information
- Nutritionist's Calories: 278 kcal 14%
- Total Fat: 13.1 g 20%
- Carbohydrates: 37.7g 12%
- Protein: 3.9 g 8%
- Cholesterol: 31 mg 10%
- Sodium: 166 mg 7%

Note Me

27. Gluten-Free Banana Bread Made Easy

"This is a great combination among pecans, nutmeg, sweet honey that I can eat this healthy bread all the tie without getting bored."

Servings: 10 | Prep: 10 m | Ready In: 1 h

Ingredients

- 3 large ripe bananas
- 1 egg
- 1 1/3 c gluten-free all-purpose baking flour
- 1/4 c honey
- 1/4 c vegetable oil
- 1/4 c flaxseed meal
- 1 tbsp. bourbon vanilla extract
- 2 1/2 tsps. baking powder
- 1 tsp. baking soda
- 1/2 tsp. xanthan gum
- 1/2 tsp. ground nutmeg
- 1 dash salt
- 1/2 c chopped pecans

Directions

- Heat the oven to 350^0F. Line parchment paper in the bottom of the loaf pan.
- Stir egg and mashed bananas in a large bowl. Blend with salt, nutmeg, xanthan gum, baking soda, baking powder, vanilla extract, flaxseed meal, oil, honey and flour. Fold in pecans and pour the batter in the lined loaf pan.
- Bring to bake for 50-60 minutes.

Nutrition Information

- Nutritionist's Calories: 237 kcal 12%
- Total Fat: 11.8 g 18%
- Carbohydrates: 32g 10%
- Protein: 3.9 g 8%
- Cholesterol: 19 mg 6%
- Sodium: 301 mg 12%

Note Me

28. Gluten-Free Vegan Banana Nut Bread

"This recipe must be the American's favorite with the ingredients of banana. Without sugar or oil, this bread is still flavorful and tasty. It is gluten free and vegan."

*Servings: 8 | **Prep:** 25 m | **Ready In:** 1 h 20 m*

Ingredients

- cooking spray
- 2 tbsps. boiling water
- 1 tbsp. flax seeds
- 1 c mashed ripe bananas
- 1/4 c unsweetened applesauce
- 2 tsps. vanilla extract
- 1 c chopped Medjool dates
- 1 c oat flour
- 1/2 c tapioca starch
- 4 tsps. baking powder
- 1 tsp. ground cinnamon
- 1/2 tsp. baking soda
- 1/2 c chopped walnuts

Directions

- Heat the oven to 350⁰F. Grease a thin layer over a 9x5 inch loaf pan with cooking spray.
- Blend flax seeds in boiling water.
- Mix vanilla extract, applesauce and bananas in a food processor and pulse until well blended. Add dates in and run the food processor. Blend with flaxseed mixture until smooth.
- Blend baking soda, cinnamon, baking powder, tapioca starch and oat flour together in a large bowl. Mix with banana mixture until a

batter forms. Add walnuts to stir and pour the batter into the loaf pan.

- Bring to bake for 55-65 minutes. Let cool in a wire rack.

Nutrition Information

- Nutritionist's Calories: 227 kcal 11%
- Total Fat: 6.8 g 10%
- Carbohydrates: 41.4g 13%
- Protein: 3.8 g 8%
- Cholesterol: 0 mg 0%
- Sodium: 261 mg 10%

Note Me

29. Grain Free Banana Bread

"This banana bread is very tasty and totally gluten-free. It is rich in fiber and protein with the ingredient of chickpeas."

Servings: *12* | **Prep:** *15 m* | **Ready In:** *1 h 30 m*

Ingredients
- 3 ripe bananas
- 1 (15 ounce) can chickpeas (garbanzo beans), drained and rinsed
- 1/2 c melted butter
- 1/2 c chopped pitted dates
- 1/2 c almond flour
- 1/4 c honey
- 4 eggs
- 1 tsp. baking soda
- 1 tsp. grated fresh ginger
- 1 tsp. ground cinnamon
- 1 tsp. vanilla extract
- 3/4 tsp. salt

Directions
- Heat the oven to 350⁰F. Grease a thin layer over a large loaf pan.
- Mix salt, vanilla extract, cinnamon, ginger, baking soda, eggs, honey, almond flour, dates, butter, chickpeas and bananas in a food processor until smooth. Transfer the batter into the loaf pan.
- Bring to bake for 1 hour and let cool in the pan for 15 minutes. Slice and serve.

Nutrition Information
- Nutritionist's Calories: 190 kcal 9%

- Total Fat: 9.7 g 15%
- Carbohydrates: 23.8g 8%
- Protein: 3.9 g 8%
- Cholesterol: 82 mg 27%
- Sodium: 399 mg 16%

Note Me

30. Honey-Spice Whole Wheat Banana Bread

"This recipe for banana bread is very moist and sweet enough to be your favorite banana bread ever. Besides, it is also very good for health."

Servings: 12 | Prep: 15 m | Ready In: 1 h 15 m

Ingredients
- 1 1/4 c walnuts
- 1 1/2 c whole wheat flour
- 1/2 c all-purpose flour
- 1 tsp. ground cinnamon
- 3/4 tsp. baking soda
- 1/2 tsp. salt
- 1/4 tsp. ground nutmeg
- 1 1/2 c mashed overripe bananas, or more to taste
- 1/2 c raw honey
- 2 eggs, lightly beaten
- 1/4 c plain yogurt
- 1/4 c coconut oil, melted and cooled
- 2 tbsps. butter, melted and cooled
- 1 tsp. vanilla extract

Directions
- Heat the oven to 350⁰F. Put walnuts on the baking sheet.
- Toast in the oven with nuts for 10-15 minutes. Chop walnuts coarsely.
- Put all walnuts in a large bowl and mix with nutmeg, salt, baking soda, cinnamon, all-purpose flour and whole wheat flour until blended well.

- Blend vanilla extract, butter, coconut oil, yogurt, eggs, honey and mashed eggs together in a large bowl. Mix the two mixtures together with a wooden spoon until well blended.
- Grease a thin layer over a 9x5 inch loaf pan. Transfer the batter into the pan which has been prepared.
- Bring to bake for 50-60 minutes.

Nutrition Information
- Nutritionist's Calories: 293 kcal 15%
- Total Fat: 16 g 25%
- Carbohydrates: 35.3g 11%
- Protein: 6.2 g 12%
- Cholesterol: 36 mg 12%
- Sodium: 206 mg 8%

Note Me

31. Janet's Famous Banana Nut Bread

"My mom has created it and until now, it is still our favorite bread. You can choose to use nuts or not. Enjoy!"

Servings: 20 | Prep: 20 m | Ready In: 1 h 25 m

Ingredients
- 3 c white sugar
- 3/4 c butter, softened
- 3 eggs
- 2 c mashed ripe banana
- 1/2 c sour cream
- 3 1/2 c all-purpose flour
- 1 tsp. baking soda
- 1/2 tsp. baking powder
- 1/2 tsp. ground cinnamon
- 1 1/2 c chopped pecans

Directions
- Heat the oven to 325^0F. Make a greasy layer and a flour layer over two 8x4 inch pans.
- Blend butter and sugar together in a large bowl until light and fluffy. Stir in eggs well one at a time and add to blend with banana and sour cream.
- Mix pecans, cinnamon, baking powder, baking soda and flour in another bowl. Add to blend with the banana mixture. Transfer the mixture into the prepared pans.
- Bring to bake for 55-65 minutes. Take out and put on a wire rack to cool. Serve warm or cold as you wish.

Nutrition Information

- Nutritionist's Calories: 356 kcal 18%
- Total Fat: 15 g 23%
- Carbohydrates: 53.3g 17%
- Protein: 4.5 g 9%
- Cholesterol: 49 mg 16%
- Sodium: 135 mg 5%

Note Me

Index

A

Allspice, *16*

Almond, *81*

Apple, *42, 53*

Apple sauce, *53*

B

Baking, *9-10, 13, 16-17, 19, 21, 23, 25, 27, 29, 32, 35, 37, 40, 42, 44, 46-47, 49, 52, 55, 57, 60, 65, 67, 69, 71, 73, 76, 78, 81, 83, 86*

Baking powder, *9, 13, 19, 21, 23, 27, 29, 37, 40, 42, 46-47, 49, 55, 57, 60, 65, 67, 71, 76, 78, 86*

Baking soda, *9, 13, 16-17, 19, 21, 23, 25, 29, 32, 35, 37, 40, 42, 44, 46-47, 49, 52, 57, 60, 65, 69, 71, 73, 76, 78, 81, 83, 86*

Banana, *9, 12-13, 16-17, 19, 21, 23, 25, 27, 29, 32, 35, 37, 40, 44, 46-47, 49, 52-53, 55, 57, 60, 63, 65, 67, 69, 71, 73, 76, 78, 81, 83, 86*

Banana bread, *9, 12, 40, 44, 49, 57, 60, 65, 76, 81, 83*

Beans, *81*

Beer, *16-17*

Biscuits, *9*

Black sesame seeds, *49*

Blueberry, *52-53, 73*

Bran, *65*

Bread, *9-13, 16, 19, 21, 23, 25, 27, 32, 35, 37, 40, 42, 44, 46-47, 49, 52, 55, 57, 60, 63, 65, 67, 69, 71, 73, 76, 78, 81, 83, 86*

Brown sugar, *16, 32, 37, 46-47, 49, 52-53, 55, 57, 60, 65*

Butter, *9, 23, 25, 27, 32, 40, 46, 52, 55, 63, 69, 71, 81, 83-84, 86*

Buttermilk, *21, 44*

C

Cake, *9, 20, 52*

Cardamom, *16-17, 57*

Cheese, *60, 71*

Chickpea, *81*

Cinnamon, *13, 16-17, 19, 29, 32, 37, 46-47, 49, 60, 78, 81, 83, 86*

Cloves, *16-17, 19*

Coconut, *46-47, 83-84*

Coconut oil, *83-84*

Coffee, *63*

Corn oil, *27*

Cranberry, *13, 37*

Cranberry sauce, *13*

Cream, *9, 60, 71, 73, 86*

Cream cheese, *60, 71*

Cream of tartar, *9*

Curd, *52*

Currants, *16*

D

Date, *16-17, 78, 81*

E

Egg, *9, 13, 16, 19, 21, 23, 25, 27, 32-33, 35, 37, 40, 42, 44, 46-47, 49, 52-53, 55, 57, 60, 63, 65, 67, 69, 71, 73, 76, 81, 83-84, 86*

Egg white, *49*

F

Fat, *9-10, 14, 17, 21, 23, 25,*
28, 30, 33, 36, 38, 41-42, 44, 47, 50, 53, 55, 58, 61, 64, 66, 68, 70-71, 74, 77, 79, 82, 84, 87

Flour, *9, 13, 16-17, 19, 21, 23, 25, 27, 29, 32, 35, 37, 40, 42, 44, 46-47, 49, 52-53, 55, 57-58, 60, 63, 65, 67, 69, 71, 73, 76, 78, 81, 83, 86*

Fruit, *9, 19, 42, 63*

G

Ginger, *16-17, 81*

Grain, *81*

H

Honey, *29, 35, 76, 81, 83-84*

L

Lemon, *46-47, 52, 67*

Lemon curd, *52*

Lemon juice, *67*

M

Macadamia, *40, 46-47*

Margarine, *60, 69*

Milk, *9, 13, 29, 46-47, 49, 65*

Conclusion

A big thanks for your downloading this book!

We really hope that you will enjoy it!

We would be really appreciated if you enjoy the book and post your reviews on Amazon.

If you do not satisfy any things in the book, please send us an email and we will reply you as soon as possible. PuPaDo Cooking Family are always looking forward to getting your contribution for our development.

Thank you!

If you need further information, **feel free to contact at:** *cooking@pupado.com*

Read More Our Cookbooks Here

365 Days Cooking With PuPaDo Family

www.pupado.com/cooking

www.amazon.com/author/pupadofamily